AF443848

Ins and Outs

of

Operations Management

3

ISBN: 9798677900877

Imprint: Independently published

This book is dedicated to those discovering operations management for the first time and desiring a quick introductory overview of the concepts and tools. Also, to those who would like a quick refresher.

6

Table of Contents

Managing Operations

Operations management is certainly one of the most important aspects of running a successful business, if not the most important. This is simply because operations management touches virtually every portion of the organization in one form or another. Anywhere within the organization there lives a process, or multiple processes to attain an outcome, operation management has responsibility. It matters very little what kind of organization is discussed, if it utilizes processes, it is employing some variation of operations management.

Organizations are basically either a for-profit or non-profit entity, and are in existence to render either a service, product, or some variation of both. Generally, there is a service piece that complements production of hard goods, and operation management can or should participate heavily in both arenas. It is taught readily that there is a good deal of differing factors when it comes to applying operations management successfully to different types of business models, and that can be demonstrated as being true, but it really comes down to some basic application goals. These application goals can easily transfer into whichever organization type one may be discussing. For instance, the focus for managing operations will be, quality, efficient use of resources, customer/stakeholder satisfaction, lean efficient processes, process improvement, measuring and maintaining smart goals, employee satisfaction/engagement, organizational culture, etc. Each of these can be broken into sub-groups and present with their own challenges. But, all operation management tools can be aptly applied to either a for-profit or non-profit entity, as well as the rendering of a service or product, without much need for special expertise beyond a common understanding of how goals are reached. It comes down to the understanding of processes and how to successfully manage those processes. One must not forget that the leadership of those who perform the processes is equally part of managing operations. "Behavioral operations is now an established and fundamental research field dedicated to understanding how the behavior of managers, workers, and customers influences operational decisions and outcomes." (Roth & Rosenzweig, 2020)

Processes

Simply put, a process is that which brings about a transformation by taking an input(s) and transforming it into a desired output. The output is either in the form of a product, or the completion of a service rendered. When we think of input, there is a great deal of things that can be categorized as an input to a process. Some examples would be raw materials, people, orders, finances, research, and/or anything that is needed to make possible the production of a finished product or completed service. In summary, we apply resources to inputs to produce a desired outcome.

Some process items can be considered both input and resource.   Money is an example of one such item. When considering finances as an input, the goal in business, of course, is to have the finished product or service generate a larger amount of dollars in return than went into the process. This is certainly a no brainer, but one has to remember that initial cost identified as input has to be added to the cost occurring in the actual process and monitored appropriately, or the goals for return on investment (ROI) may be inadvertently reduced, or be absent all together. Input cost can be static, but process cost is most usually dynamic in nature.

The process(s) is the key focus of operations management and needs to be understood thoroughly in order to make changes that move toward lean, efficient operation. Lean, efficient operation that produces all desired aspects and goals of the product and/or service outcomes is not only ideal, it is essential to competing in today's business arena. Every item and activity that are part of the process flow must be scrutinized for necessity and optimum contribution. "Finding the best combination of elements is the mission of organization." (Schroeder, Nebl, & Mainzinger, 2014) Waste must be reduced to absolute minimum, and contribution and efficiency must be enhanced to the maximum degree. In order to accomplish this type of performance, every individual piece and activity of the process must be understood by itself, as well as how it participates and impacts the process flow toward the outcome.

The customer is the reason for operations, and a good process of operation is one that produces a service or product that meets, or better yet, exceeds the customer's expectations. The best way to meet the needs of the organization and its stakeholders, is to exceed the expectations of its customers in the most efficient, cost effective way possible. This brings into consideration things like process flexibility that allows customization, product cost to the customer, and the speed of production and delivery, among others. There is a great deal that goes into developing optimum processes. It is what makes operations management a challenging endeavor, and the need for being an area of expertise unto itself.

Operations Frontier Strategy

When we think of strategy in relation to operations management, we are speaking of designing operations around, and based on a thorough understanding of the corporate strategic plan, or goal. Some organizations are complex and multifaceted in terms of services and/or products offered, while others are narrower and more focused on one, or a handful of offerings. Any given corporation may have a structure that involves many different business units under the main goal. This means specific competencies need designed for each process existing within the business units. As the operations strategy is developed, circumstances such as the organization's performance in comparison to its competition, and the various trade-offs that will exist must be taken into consideration. "In competitive markets, the operations strategies of companies are normally formulated based on their competitive advantages..." (Kaviani, & Abbasi, 2014) It is not practical to believe one can have the best of every variable existing throughout every process. The assessment, understanding, and determination of these circumstances can be demonstrated in what is termed the operations frontier.

To demonstrate a typical trade-off, one makes in designing processes and competencies, a simple graph can be utilized to aid understanding. If we take a process attribute such as flexibility and place it on the Y axis, and another such as efficiency and place it at the same distance out on the X axis, then draw the curve connecting the two positions on the graph, we have represented the operations frontier with the curved line. This means the closer one moves toward the attribute of flexibility on the frontier, the less efficient the process will be. The trade-off to offer a more flexible process that allows added customization for the customer, is the cost of a less efficient process. One might assume that being directly in the center of the frontier between efficiency and flexibility is the ideal place for their process to reside. That rarely proves to be true, however. The ideal positioning on the operations frontier should be directly related to customer preference, satisfaction, and the competition's position on the frontier. This, of course, must remain in conjunction with and align appropriately alongside profitability. The one thing that is sure, being located inside the curve representing the frontier means the process is not optimum regarding any attribute, and resides below performance levels of other organizations.

To better articulate this concept, I will visit an actual scenario from my personal experience in the health care industry. I will use patient scheduling as an example. In a service line, it was far more efficient to control patient scheduling by assigning time slots for patients throughout an eight-hour day that had them arriving consecutively without time gaps between appointments. This would allow for the most cost-efficient way to utilize staffing to care for the patients. This meant that while staffing was on site, they were continually caring for patients and producing revenue with no wasted time expenditure. However, this also meant that as patients were added to the agenda, they were forced to attend therapy sessions during the next available time slot whether it was convenient for them or not. An organization could continue this approach to scheduling if they so desired, as long as there was no other option for patients from competing entities.

If a competitor offering the same service decided they would sacrifice efficiency to offer schedule flexibility for patients, with the goal of wooing patients to their program, then some decisions must be made. In this example the competitor has decided the trade-off of efficiency for flexibility will serve them better by drawing patients to their program, as they provide a better patient experience. They are willing to accept added cost to gain business and improve their market position. The competition's overall goal is to become the preferred provider. The hope is that being the preferred provider will eventually eliminate their cost inefficiency by having their program slots filled on a regular basis and making wasted time nonexistent. The original organization must then decide if it is in their best interest to move toward an efficiency trade-off that equals the position of the competition. They must calculate if they can afford such a move, and if it is worth doing so to retain current customers and remove any advantage the competitor will gain moving forward.

There are a variety of attributes to be considered as aforementioned when designing and maintaining operations at an optimum performance level. An additional example might be product quality versus time of product to customer. It is important to remember that managing operations is a dynamic undertaking and is never without room for improvement and/or process tweaking.

Process Structure

As I discuss process structure, I am referring to how an individual process is constructed from its beginning point to its end. When designing a process, the first thing needed is to assess what competencies will be satisfied and what attributes are necessary. This means items like cost, production time, customization flexibility, and quality level, among others, are to be determined up front.

There are a couple of different process structure types I will mention here beginning with what is termed "Job Shop" architecture. In this type of process architecture, there is flexibility built in that allows for the customization of product. The resources such as equipment are capable of general purpose and can be used in a variety of ways to produce different products, or variations to products fairly easy. An example of this would be a programmable CNC lathe machine that can be set up to produce any number of different sized and/or type of machined parts as customer orders come in. This particular process architecture is an example of choosing flexibility over cost effectiveness that is recognized as a trade-off like that which was spoken of earlier. It is also notorious for increased process flow times.

The next process structure type is termed "Flow Shop" and is designed for a specific type of production that does not incorporate flexibility into the architecture. This process structure brings to mind what can be viewed as an assembly line, where the same activities are repeated consistently to produce the same product as quickly and efficiently at a particular quality level as possible. This process structure is best at delivering cost effectiveness and the shortest flow times. One aspect of the two structure types that needs mentioned is that the human capital is utilized differently for each. The Job Shop design is producing a variety of customized products on complex machines that require a higher level of trained personnel than does the Flow Shop structure, where employees are required to provide repetitive assembly line type activity. This adds cost to the Job

Shop architecture and reduces cost for the Flow Shop designed processes.

There is a process structure that falls in between the Job Shop and the Flow Shop termed the "Batch Shop" architecture. It can utilize and emphasize any aspects or attributes of the Job or flow shop structures needed to produce the desired outcome. It can be thought of as incorporating flexibility into the process flow to alter production in order to produce a product until a predetermined number of the product is produced. The process is then switched over to another product type until its desired number is produced creating "batches" of products. "Process structure and product newness require different… configurations, which change as products mature…" (Tsinopoulos, & Mena, 2015)

24

Auditing Operations

Keeping in mind the strategy and overall goal of the organization, operations auditing helps make sure the business is continually heading in the right direction and producing the desired outcomes. Areas of interest to keep an eye on, along with processes, are marketing and finance. Auditing is the act of examining current capabilities of in-place processes and determining if adjustments are needed to realign what is currently happening with what the organization desires to accomplish. This should definitely take precedence when coming into, starting, or acquiring a new business. It must also occur continually throughout the life of the business to insure continued effectiveness and viability.

When auditing operations, it is necessary to have a thorough understanding of strategic market position regarding your own organization, as well as that of the competing entities. When determining needed adjustments to current process structure that will achieve organizational goals, it must be understood that moving the organization to an optimum strategic position that supersedes the competition's positioning is the focus. One way to remain or become viable, is to produce an equal or higher quality product or service more efficiently with greater cost effectiveness. "How can we improve product quality and yield? More than ever, the answer to this question is vital as product life cycles are getting shorter and international competition is getting keener. Since this question arises repeatedly when a new product is developed, quality improvement should be achieved faster and in a more systematic way." (Kano & Nakagawa, 2008) Another way to achieve viability is creating a niche in the marketplace that gains advantage by producing a product or service that is utterly unique. If it can be determined how to add a greater amount of customization to the product or service, and still be able to afford the cost of production while generating an acceptable return on investment, it will greatly enhance the possibility of a superior strategic market position.

Fitting into the Strategic Plan

This is where determination is needed to produce and monitor how well the process development and competence of the organization results in proper desired market position. Does the product or service line up with the business strategy regarding its market position and comparison to competing organizations and circumstantial factors? Does it stand up to market drivers and obstacles successfully?

Regarding strategies, a market-driven strategy is simply a strategy based on assuring desired market position is obtained by the product or service attributes. Some examples might be related to the choice of being the lowest cost provider, or perhaps the highest quality provider. It might be that variety in customization is needed to outmaneuver the competition. The market-driven strategy then decides process development goals. A process-driven strategy, on the other hand, takes into account what processes and competencies are already in place that can be capitalized upon to create a desired market placement that rivals competing entities.

These are two perspectives that be chosen for various reasons. One being financial. If the processes in place are sufficient to achieve a highly strategic market position, then this will prove far more cost effective than creating new process competencies from scratch to achieve the desired position. It is reasonable to believe that it is not practical to try and develop processes that will be able to accomplish all possible desired outcomes. Choices will need to be made regarding trade-offs based on the most pertinent and accurate data available. It is usually dependent on what will produce the greatest ROI and stakeholder alignment.

Sometimes it is decided that the bottom line is slightly discarded in order to steel market position. This is with the hope of crowding out the competition and gaining a better footprint that increases viability and profitability in the long run. This is if the bottom line can take the hit and the desired results are highly probable.

Smart Goals and Metrics Monitoring

Once it is felt the right processes are created and proper strategic fit is understood and engaged, a way to ensure it is working properly and continues to achieve the organizational goals must be put in place. This is where smart goals and metrics measures come into play. "Using specific, measurable, achievable, realistic/relevant, and tangible/time-bound (SMART) criteria in goal setting works well when the goal is to improve an existing system about which much is known." (Prather, 2005) Based on desired outcomes and customer expectations, specific aspects of the process or processes must be monitored and measured. These chosen aspects must be ones that are not influenced or determined by uncontrollable outside factors.

An example might be that time is a concern if the process is one that possesses a certain amount of customization flexibility. It would be prudent then to track and monitor the time required to change equipment over to produce a different variation of the product or service. If overall cost is a concern it may be that waste and or production downtime is monitored to determine and maintain acceptable variance. Quality control is a typical concern and measured to keep the production of defective units to a minimum and acceptable amount. The more points of monitoring within a process will lead to the most efficient and cost-effective outcomes that meet customer and stakeholder demands. One piece that can be monitored for inspiring continued improvement is customer complaints.

It should be understood that price, market share, and sales are not a part of the process metrics. For whatever reason this is sometimes a point on confusion. Price for example, is not necessarily directly related the cost of manufacture. Price is driven by many outside influencers and circumstances. The same is true of market share and sales, they are affected by many external factors.

Once it has been determined what metrics will be measured and monitored, real and practical goals must be set for the measuring and monitoring to be weighed against. This is where the utilization of standard deviation concepts can be very beneficial in determining what is actually occurring vs. what is desired to happen. Once a desired target is set, the process can be continually monitored for accuracy, and prompt pursuit of corrective actions when processes are failing to be in alignment.

Analyzing the Process

Operations management is studied from a process view. When viewing an organization, it is a culmination of interconnected events that lead to product production or service fulfillment. When an order comes in everything that happens to get the order complete and to the customer can be seen as one big process. The truth of the matter, of course, is that there exist numerous interrelated smaller processes that all have the potential to be optimized.

The goal is to figure out from the moment when an order is received, how can the process time be reduced to its shortest possibility, the highest level of cost effectiveness be obtained, while producing the greatest measure of quality. The only way to accomplish this is to fully understand the process and examine each step to determine the value added. Anything that does not add value to the outcome should be removed or improved. Things like equipment downtime, or time waiting for something else to occur can be considered non-valuable additions to the process.

If all is occurring as desired a process can be considered as stable. This is when the average inflow equals the average outflow. We speak in averages because it is certain that fluctuations within the process will occur. The best that can be achieved is maintaining tight averages that produce within a particular target range.

Three process variables create a starting place for what must be measured to ensure a stable process. The first of these is flow time. This is tracking how long it takes to get a unit through the process from start to finish on average. The next is inventory. This is how many units are in process at any given time on average. The third is assessing throughput rate. This is knowing on average how many units are entering the process vs. how many are going out at the same time. The reason these three variables are considered important operational measures, is based on the fact that they can be connected. It can be understood in terms of what is known as "Little's Law". The Little's Law formula is expressed as such: Avg. Inventory = Throughput Rate X Avg. Flow Time (I = R X T). With this formula, it can be calculated whether or not a process is meeting the average goals determined appropriate for each of these variables in the process.

The Little's Law formula can be applied to the financial data of an organization as well, using information obtained from the balance sheet or income statement. Sometimes the financial data is easier to refer to than process specifics. This is done by tracking dollars as they move through the process.

Inventory (I) is an obvious value and listed in the financial data as a dollar amount. Flow rate (R) is understood as dollars put into the process and related to "cost of goods sold", listed as a dollar amount in the financial data. Now that we have these two values plunged into the formula, we can determine the time variable (T) as follows, T=I/R. The answer will result in dollars per year. For example, if we end up with .134 years, multiply the result by 52 weeks and we end up with how many weeks it takes 1 dollar put in, to become 1 dollar out that is able to be billed to the customer. In this case we arrive at 6.968 weeks. If this is within our predetermined goal for the process, we can relax for the time being, if not, it is time for a deep dive investigation as to why not.

Flow Diagrams

The tool of choice for representing and breaking down processes is the Flow diagram. Flow diagrams are used to display exactly step by step what is occurring within a process from start to finish.

The first thing to become familiar with are the four key symbols that make up a flow diagram. A rectangle is used to represent activity, triangles represent areas of waiting, arrows show direction of flow, and a circle represent the start and stop points. Adhering to the proper use of these symbols allows anyone with a knowledge of flow diagrams to easily track and understand the flow and content of a process.

When constructing a flow diagram, it is vital to include the concept of precedence. This simply means that all activities occur in the order they must happen. It must be easily seen which activities must preceded other activities before they can occur. For example, the gathering of supplies must occur in the diagram before anything can actually be shown occurring to or with the supplies. Some activities may have multiple actions that must occur prior to their occurring, and this must be accurately represented in order. Sometimes it is helpful to list precedence in a table along with a diagram, to spell out what activities have actions that must preceded them and what the actions are. This can be used to add more detail.

Depending on the complexity of any given process, once it has been displayed in diagram form, there may be a number of different paths that can be followed throughout the process from start to finish. This is because there is the possibility of actions taking place simultaneously throughout the process. Each path will contribute its own amount of time to reach completion from start to finish. The path that takes the longest to complete is considered the "Critical Path".

It is important to understand the critical path and its relationship to the overall process for multiple reasons. The first thing to note is that, as long as the other paths of actions do not break down in a way that results in time delays that become longer than the time it takes for the critical path to be completed, and does not cause delay in the critical path itself, the process will still be completed on time. Also, if the other paths are completed on time or early, it may be possible to redirect resources to the critical path to speed the completion time of the overall process.

Another way to understand the relationship of the critical path to its process is in terms of "Slack Time". Because there are paths that require less time to complete, there is room for delay. This means that not all process paths must be started exactly on time. Instead, attention can be given to the critical path if and when needed, to make sure it remains timely and on track. This will again, ensure the overall process time is not delayed.

Efficiency

"In the global economy and in business administration science, the interest in process-oriented organization and management has increased significantly since the 1990s." (Fauser & Heidrich, 2018) Once we have a developed process, have it broken down by activity in a flow diagram, and have determined the critical path, we can assess and calculate the process efficiency. When determining the efficiency of a process, each activity has an efficiency that needs calculated. This is done by monitoring each activity under ideal conditions to record the exact time needed to complete each activity. Ideal conditions imply that the activity time is derived when all supplies are at hand, all actions occur properly without delay, and nothing influences the activity in an adverse way. In other words, a perfect world scenario. This is referred to as the "Theoretical Time". Once this time is arrived at, then each process activity should be monitored over an appropriate amount of time to determine the average time it takes to accomplish each activity under real world conditions. On any given day, an activity can take longer or shorter due to unexpected influences and/or delays. Once this average time is known for each activity within the process, efficiency can be calculated as such, Theoretical time ÷ Actual time × 100. This will provide an efficiency percentage for each activity.

Now that we understand the efficiency of each activity based on our calculations, we need to determine which activity to focus improvement measures toward to improve the overall process. It may seem that all low efficiency activities would be a target for improvement, and should be if they are producing waste and adding to process cost, but the main focus should be narrower.

In order to find where improvement to efficiency would serve us best, we need to return to the path we decided was the critical path, based on the longer time it takes to complete from start to finish in the process. We may be able to easily improve an activity within a path that is not part of the critical path, but because the critical path takes longer to complete regardless of this improvement, the overall efficiency has not been affected. The process time from start to finish will remain the same based on the critical path.

The way to improve the process is to focus attention on the lowest efficiency activity within the critical path first. Once that has been dealt with, one can move on to the next least efficient activity within the critical path, and so on. Should the critical path be improved to the point it is no longer the most time-consuming path, then a new critical path is established. Focus should then be aimed at the least efficient activity in the new critical path until all activities in the new critical path are as efficient as possible. This process of improving activity efficiency should be taken as far as it can be, until all options are exhausted.

Capacity

An additional characteristic of a process that must be understood and monitored, as well as effectively managed, is process capacity. When process capacity is discussed, it is in terms of how many completed units are produced in any given amount of time. For instance, how many units are completed per hour. The inverse can then be arrived at also, as how many minutes it takes for a unit to come out of the process completed. In other words, if ten units come out per hour then a unit is completed every six minutes. This is not to be confused with how long it takes a unit to pass through the entire process.

The process capacity is needed and useful to monitor process consistency and its ability to meet customer demand. The process capacity is termed "Takt Time". The takt time can also be found in relation to the longest activity time occurring within the process. If the longest activity time is twenty minutes, the takt time is twenty minutes. The takt time for customer demand can be determined as follows. If it is known that we have a customer demand of 40 units per day, and we work one shift per day for eight hours, we find the takt time by dividing the amount of time we have available for processing by the number of units needed. $8 \div 40 = .2 \times 100$. This reveals that a unit must come out of the process completed every twenty minutes. With this information it can be decided if the process will be sufficient for meeting demand, or if it is necessary to make additional provisions. This could be in the form of additional processing time, resources, or duplicating the entire process to double production, etc.

Profitability is an important element of concern in relation to process efficiency and can be predicted with the data derived from process capacity. When the profit generated per unit is calculated, it is easy to figure and monitor profit based on the possible and actual process capacity. This is simply done by multiplying the process capacity times the profit per unit for a given period of time. If the profit per unit is 5 dollars and we make 40 units per day, our profit is $5 \times 40 = 200$ dollars per day. This will result in 1000 dollars per week and 52000 dollars per year, and so on. This is, of course, if process cost does not fluctuate and all goes according to plan.

Inventory

When looking at inventory, there are a number of things to consider as to its impact and usefulness within the process. There are three types of inventory to understand. The first being "Input Inventory". This of course, refers to the items that will be entering the process. Inventory that is within the process, passing through activities or waiting within the process is the "In-Process Inventory". And, naturally, items that have been completed by the process awaiting shipment to the customer, or to the next process is "Output Inventory". Adding these three types of inventory together gives us "Total Inventory".

One useful aspect of inventory within a process is to act as a buffer. It creates a slight separation of processes so if one is running slower than another, the faster process does not need to stop and wait for the slower process. Inventory can be allowed to build up in preparation for the next process.

In addition, inventory can be a tool for spreading fixed cost over inventory quantity as associated with economies of scale. For example, if there is a fixed cost from product design that was incurred once, it is spread over how many items are built up in inventory. If a customer buys 1000 units, the design cost and any other fixed cost can be seen as spread over that number of units. This causes the individual unit cost to go down.

In regard to production, process capacity, and customer demand, allowing inventory to build up can ensure that during times of delay, lack of resources, or breakdowns, customer demand can still be met if there is adequate inventory stored up to fall back on until normal operations resume. It can also be used in this way to smooth out fluctuating demand by allowing inventory to increase or decrease. Seasonal product demand being an example.

Another aspect of inventory to be concerned with is price maintenance. If a product or resource is predicted to rise in cost in the near future that will add cost to the production, it may be prudent buy a larger quantity of the product now to avoid higher cost for the future.

It should also be remembered that inventory comes with a cost of its own in the way of inventory storage. Warehouse cost, cost of tracking inventory, possible need for climate control, etc. need to be taken into account when monitoring and making inventory decisions. Another cost associated with inventory worthy of concern, is opportunity cost. Monies tied up in inventory is money that cannot be invested in other projects or interests.

The inventory annual total cost equation is an important part of understanding the financial impact of inventory within the operations of an organization. It provides the knowledge of how much of an item to order at any given time. The annual total cost consists of three main components. 1) The cost of ordering inventory per year. 2) The cost of maintaining inventory per year. 3) The actual cost off the inventory itself. Maintaining inventory includes the physical cost to store and/or transport inventory, as well as that associated with opportunity cost.

In order to analyze total inventory cost, there are several variables that are involved. First, one must have knowledge of the number of units ordered at any given time (Quantity). Also, the annual through put rate per year (Rate). Next the cost to acquire one unit is needed (Cost). Next in line would be the set-up cost (Set-up Cost). This is considered the fixed cost associated with order placement each time an order is placed. Additionally, the holding cost as a percentage of the unit cost is needed (Physical Holding Cost). Next is the opportunity cost as a percentage of the unit cost (Opportunity Cost). Finally, the annual holding cost of an individual unit (H) expressed as H = (physical holding cost + opportunity cost) × cost.

So, to determine annual set-up cost, the following equation is applied, (set-up cost × rate) ÷ quantity. To arrive at the annual holding cost, the following equation is used, (H × quantity) ÷ 2. Annual cost of units purchased can be found with the equation, cost × rate.

This means that the total annual cost equals set-up cost + annual holding cost + annual cost of units purchased.

Next it is necessary to discuss what is referred to as "Economic Order Quantity" (EOQ). This is the process by which the most cost-effective amount to order at any given time throughout the year is determined. I will give a broad overview of the concept because of the nature of the process. The reason for this is because the calculations are based on a perfect world scenario view. In other words, it is assumed that there are never any fluctuations in events such as customer demand, through put rate, delivery time, etc. It is assumed that everything always happens the same without any problems or delays. So basically, EOQ gives a reasonable target and not a matter of fact determination.

The items at play are set-up cost, which is cost of ordering, and holding cost, which is the cost associated with storing what we order as aforementioned. The thing to determine is how does reducing set-up cost impact holding cost. For instance, if we order units quarterly, four times per year, and our set-up cost is $1,500.00 per order, then we could save money by ordering double the amount bi-annually at a cost of $3,000.00 per year instead of at the cost of $6,000.00 when placing orders four times per year. If we do this, it needs to be compared with how holding cost will be affected by having to store and track larger quantities on hand twice per year, as opposed to lesser quantities on hand four times per year. If holding cost increase is less than the savings incurred by ordering more at a time, bi-annual ordering should be pursued. The best way to decide how many units to order each time, is to determine at what time interval and what unit amount causes set-up cost and holding cost to be equal. Ordering that number of units, that many times per year, would be the most cost-efficient option.

Something to keep in mind when figuring and implementing the most economic ordering quantity, is discounts, and/or price breaks, that are often offered by a supplier for ordering a certain amount of product each ordering cycle. If the minimum quantity to order attached to the discount falls in a range that does not adversely affect the cost of ordering and inventory maintenance/storage, then it is a cost strategy that should be considered. It also needs to be within reasonable alignment to customer demand. It is not prudent to have inventory continually piling up each ordering cycle to receive a price break that will eventually cost more in having too much inventory on hand in the long run.

When determining how much inventory to order, it is also necessary to know when it is time to reorder. The reorder point is associated with an amount of time referred to as the "Lead Time Demand". This is defined as the amount of time between when the order is placed, and when it is received. As mentioned earlier, it is not prudent to have too much Inventory on hand, but it is necessary to have enough on hand to allow for variations in the lead time. It would not be desirable to run out of inventory before the new supply arrives, causing avoidable downtime.

The amount of inventory kept on hand for the purpose of maintaining production is termed, "Safety Stock". Keeping in mind that lead time is variable, a standard deviation of lead time is used when calculating how much safety stock to keep on hand. For a simple example, if it is determined that 100 units are used during a lead time that has a standard deviation of 10, then reordering when stock is down to 110 units would be expected to keep production in play.

Product Quality

A simple definition of quality in relation to product or service, is the ability of any product or service to meet or exceed the expectations of the customer. Exceeding expectations is the goal and should be more common than just meeting a customer's expectations. Product/service quality is important as it highly impacts organizational reputation. Product reliability is directly related to customer loyalty and new customer recruitment. "…business success is tied to the ability to foster customer loyalty. Businesses that deliver superior value derived from excellent services and quality products are likely to win customer loyalty…" (Otim & Grover, 2017) Also, organizational liability can come into play with malfunctioning or defective products causing injury, or loss to the customer. This can add up to high unexpected costs for the company. It does not take long for word of mouth and/or headlines, to kill a product or company and remove them from a marketplace. On a global scale, the quality of a product must be consistent and able to compete successfully with like products or services.

Considering process improvement, reducing variations in a process and/or product leads to cost effectiveness. There are costs typically associated with quality such as, prevention of problems, product appraisal, identifying internal product failure before it reaches the customer, and external recovery cost when a problematic product reaches the customer. The latter is the worst-case scenario. Not only are you accruing costs by having to rectify the situation, but the impact on customer satisfaction and company reputation are sometimes irreversible.

There is an overall quality improvement process that is aimed at minimizing process impairments and product insufficiency. This process includes measuring, analyzing, controlling, improving, and redesigning. This is where the implementation of Six Sigma is brought into the improvement process. The key to Six Sigma is in defining a problem, measuring the variables, analyzing the data, making improvements, and controlling the processes to ensure they stay within the new specifications. This is to result in achieving the highest level of quality and cost effectiveness. There are seven tools considered to be applicable in implementing the aforementioned aspects of the Six Sigma improvement process.

Check sheets are a simple structured tool for gathering data. Check sheets are best suited for high frequency data. The check sheet is generally a list of events or activities where the frequency of occurrence is being tracked. This is accomplished by checking, or marking down how many times each tracked activity occurs within a time frame, days, hours, etc.

A scatter plot diagram (Appendix A) is useful for analyzing the relationship between two variables. It is a graph with an X and Y axis. The two variables each occupy either the X or Y axis. This results in a scattered pattern on the graph and gives a visual representation of the variables relation to each other. This is a useful tool for identifying positive or negative trends.

Pareto charts (Appendix B) are basically bar graphs designed left to right with the largest bar on the left, and the bars decreasing in size/value as it moves to the right. The vertical axis contains target values, while the horizontal axis represents items of interest. It is useful to determine what item is causing the largest problem or contributing the most or least to particular target goals.

A histogram (Appendix C) is simply a representation of the variation and/or distribution of particular data. Data is placed into categories and a graph derived from the data. All histogram data must be numerical. It is used to identify normal or abnormal distribution of data. It gives indication to whether it is necessary to compare and consider outputs across a process or processes.

Cause and effect diagrams (Appendix D), also known as fish-bone diagrams are graphical techniques used to discover causes of problems. The graph is a structured way to examine a problem. Each portion of a process is represented with possible causes of a particular adverse outcome. It simply guides identification of a problem's source so corrections can be considered and implemented.

A flow diagram (Appendix E) is one of the seven tools of quality and was addressed earlier in this work. I will not make effort to cover the subject again here except to say, it is a tool for analyzing a process from start to finish in detail.

Statistical process control is a way to monitor processes after improvements, adjustments, and/or corrective action has taken place. There is always what is considered to be normal process variation. Abnormal variation is what statistical process control is trying to identify and control. An abnormal variation is one that can be isolated to a particular cause that can be corrected. Using control charts to track data over time with predetermined parameters, helps determine between normal and abnormal variations. This is where examining the standard deviation of sample data is utilized. Six Sigma is characterized by three standard deviations above and three below the sample mean. If all variation falls within these standard deviations, then we have an efficient process. If not, process improvement is indicated, and the variation cause is likely to be external to the process.

Application

When entering an organization as the newly appointed director of operations, the following is a suggested course of action. The first thing one might do is gather an exhaustive list of policy and procedures active within the organization. This will give an initial starting point and estimate of the task ahead.

Next it would be necessary to separate out all policy and procedures that are not related to revenue producing production or services. These will be the most pertinent to attack first. Any other policy and procedures that may have cost related activities can be addressed after the chosen mountain has been climbed, or if they rise to the surface with obvious need for attention.

Moving forward, it would be time to gather the entire management team together, schedule a monthly meeting for this group, explain the goals to the gathered team related to operations management, and gain understanding of what manager and department, or section own each policy and procedure. At the end of this meeting it should be clear to the director of operations which managers own oversight of which policy and procedures, and managers should have clear understanding of their role moving forward.

After this meeting has occurred successfully, weekly meetings should be implemented with each manager for a "one on one" workshop with the director of operations. During this scheduled time, the manager will be assigned the task of picking one process under their supervision to develop into a working flow chart, and have it prepared to bring to the next weekly meeting, along with a full explanation of the process in detail. During the next weekly meeting when the information has been relayed by the manager, and the director of operations has full understanding of the process, the manager will be asked for their opinion regarding possible inefficiencies that may exist within the process that can be immediately addressed. Regardless of what is learned during this second meeting, the manager's assignment for the next meeting will be to pull their team together that participate in the hands-on application of the process, and get the team's feedback on each activity within the process. They should be looking for anything that is causing issues with efficiency or things that do not add value, whether they feel it can be improved upon or not. The information gathered will then be brought to the next weekly meeting to be relayed to the director of operations in detail.

The next assignment for the manager for the next scheduled weekly meeting time slot, will be to have his team available for a group meeting with themselves and the director of operations. This will preferably occur in the actual work area while work is under way, allowing for the director of operations to observe the process firsthand and to discuss its components with the team and the manager together as things happen. The next scheduled meeting should be a meeting with the manager to discuss what has been learned thus far, and to plan next steps in addressing any issues that have been uncovered. During the process of the above data gathering with the manager and their team, the director of operations should be assessing the information about the process they are working with to determine the appropriateness of process structure, and how well it fits into the organization's strategic plan. It is also time to be considering how it compares with the processes of competing organizations. Weekly meetings with the manager should continue consistently to keep dialogue frequent about progress.

Once any initial process improvements have been implemented, the next assignment for the manager is to develop smart goals and metric measuring to maintain consistency of the adjusted process and determine any other outliers that may be present or that materialize. The monitoring should consist of tools outlined previously in this work. The development of the monitoring process should be aided and guided by the director of operations.

The above process should, of course, be applied and carried out for each manager, and each process under each manager's oversight individually until all processes have had an initial assessment, improvement plan implemented, and monitoring put in place. For the next monthly meeting with all managers, each manager should be able to share what they have discovered, what changes have been implemented, and the impact the changes have had on productivity, cost savings, and customer satisfaction.

There will most likely be processes that are simple enough to assess without the full undertaking previously described. It is important to remember the cost being added by the analysis process, and not waste unnecessary resources and human capital on obvious circumstances. Once everything has been assessed and being monitored for consistent outcomes, it is time to start looking at extraordinary measures to induce higher levels of efficiency and quality. This might be in the form of new technologies, better equipment, alternative suppliers, outsourcing and the like. All said and done, the pursuit of improvement and ongoing movement toward leaner and more efficient processes that produce the highest quality outcomes possible, should never cease.

Appendix A

Scatter Plot Diagram

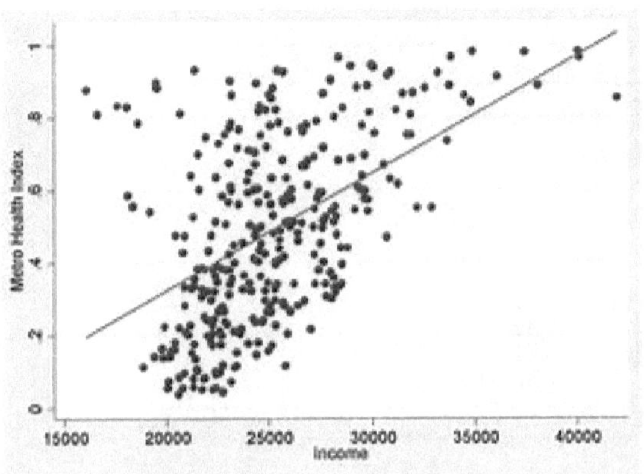

Appendix B

Pareto Chart

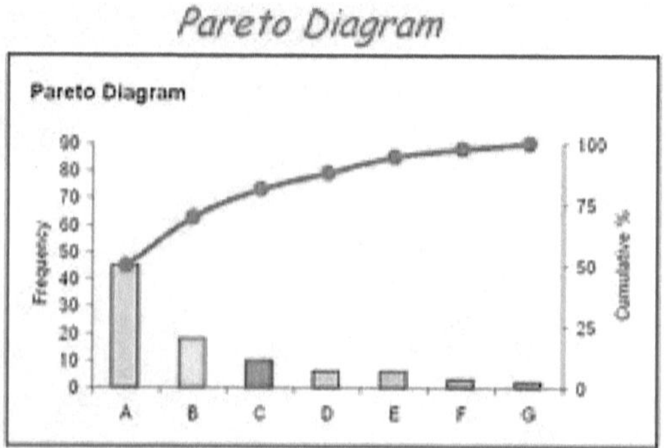

Appendix C

Histogram

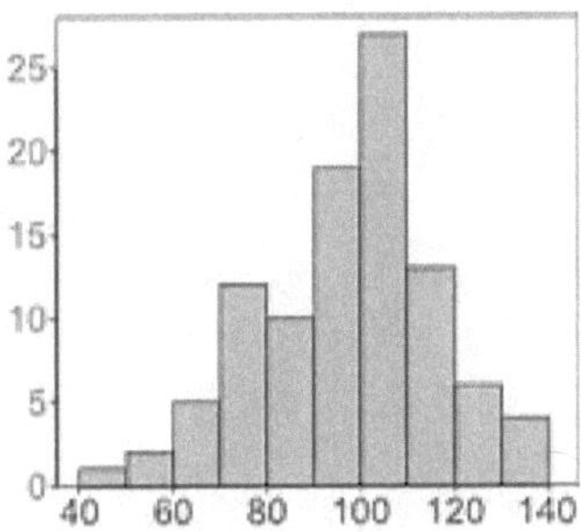

Appendix D

Cause and Effect Diagram

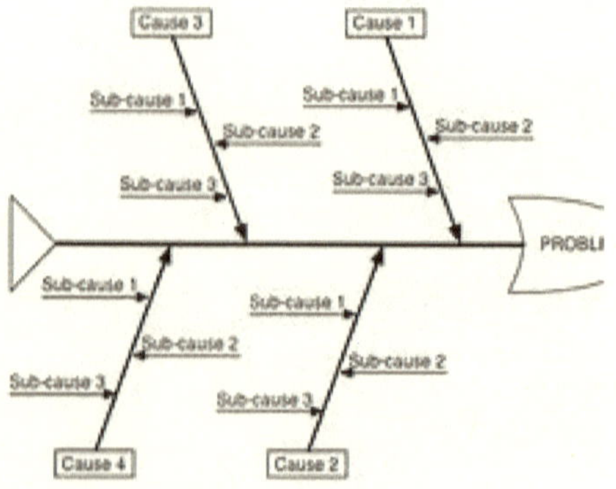

Appendix E

Flow Chart

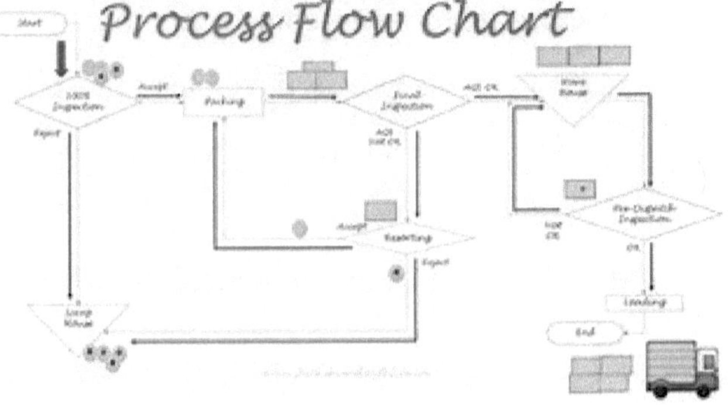

References:

Fauser, S., & Heidrich, F. (2018). The business process optimization of offer management for investment goods in individual production – the case of a german medium-sized company. *Problems and Perspectives in Management, 16*(3), 406-422. doi:http://dx.doi.org.ezproxy.liberty.edu/10.21511/ppm.16(3).2018.32

Kano, M., & Nakagawa, Y. (2008). Data-based process monitoring, process control, and quality improvement: Recent developments and applications in steel industry. *Computers & Chemical Engineering, 32*(1-2), 12-24. doi:10.1016/j.compchemeng.2007.07.005

Kaviani, M. A., & Abbasi, M. (2014). Analyzing the operations strategies of manufacturing firms using a hybrid grey DEA approach - A case of fars cement companies in iran. *International Journal of Supply and Operations Management, 1*(3), 371-391.

Otim, S., & Grover, V. (2017;2006;). An empirical study on web-based services and customer loyalty. *European Journal of Information Systems, 15*(6), 527-541. doi:10.1057/palgrave.ejis.3000652

Prather, C. W. (2005). THE DUMB THING ABOUT SMART GOALS FOR INNOVATION. *Research Technology Management, 48*(5), 14-15. Retrieved from http://ezproxy.liberty.edu/login?qurl=https%3A%2F%2Fsearch.proquest.com%2Fdocview%2F213802690%3Faccountid%3D12085

Roth, A., & Rosenzweig, E. (2020). Advancing empirical science in operations management research: A clarion call to action. *Manufacturing & Service Operations Management, 22*(1), 179-190. doi:10.1287/msom.2019.0829

Schroeder, A., Nebl, T., & Mainzinger, C. (2014). Theoretical foundations of efficiently organizing production processes: Using the example of combining organizational forms of component manufacture and internal transport. *Journal of Industrial Engineering (Hindawi), 2014*, 1-27. doi:10.1155/2014/513190

Tsinopoulos, C., & Mena, C. (2015). Supply chain integration configurations: Process structure and product newness. *International Journal of Operations & Production Management, 35*(10), 1437-1459. doi:10.1108/ijopm-08-2013-0369